COTTON

Millicent E. Selsam

Photographs by Jerome Wexler

William Morrow and Company
New York   1982

Printed in the United States of America.
1 2 3 4 5 6 7 8 9 10

Library of Congress Cataloging in Publication Data

Selsam, Millicent Ellis, 1912-
    Cotton.

    Includes index.
    Summary: Surveys the history, growth cycle, processing, and varied uses of one of the world's most important fiber plants.
    1. Cotton—Juvenile literature. 2. Cotton manufacture—Juvenile literature. [1. Cotton]
I. Wexler, Jerome, ill. II. Title.
SB249.S48   633.5'1   82-6496
ISBN 0-688-01499-2 AACR2
ISBN 0-688-01500-X (lib. bdg.)

Design by Christine Kettner

Photo Credits

All photographs are by Jerome Wexler with the exception of the following: The American Museum of Natural History, pp. 7 (J. Bird, photographer), 9 (J. Kirschner, photographer), 38 (H.S. Rice, photographer); Burlington Industries, Inc., p. 46; The Metropolitan Museum of Art, pp. 8 (Fletcher Fund, 1959), 10 (Rogers Fund, 1927); National Cotton Council of America, pp. 40, 41, 42, 43 both, 44 both, 45; Smithsonian Institution, pp. 13, 14; Millicent E. Selsam, p. 23; U.S. Department of Agriculture, pp. 34, 37, 39 top (Soil Conservation Service, B. W. Anderson, photographer), 39 bottom (David F. Warren, photographer). Permission is gratefully acknowledged.

By Millicent E. Selsam and Jerome Wexler

The Amazing Dandelion
The Apple and Other Fruits
Bulbs, Corms, and Such
Eat the Fruit, Plant the Seed
The Harlequin Moth, Its Life Story
Maple Tree
Mimosa, The Sensitive Plant
Peanut
Plants We Eat
Play With Plants
Popcorn
Vegetables from Stems and Leaves

For Connie Epstein,
with appreciation for her many years
of helpful editing

The author and the photographer wish to thank
Dr. Paul A. Fryxell, Research Botanist of the United States
Department of Agriculture, for checking the text
and photographs of this book.
They would also like to thank Doyle K. Needham,
Manager of Special Technical Projects,
of the National Cotton Council of America,
for his kind cooperation in locating photographs
for the processing section of the book.

CONTENTS

1. Discovery 7
2. The Plant 15
3. Processing 38
   Index 48

DISCOVERY

Nobody seems to know exactly when people first began to use cotton, but there is evidence that it was cultivated in India and Pakistan five thousand years ago.

During this same period, cotton also was being cultivated halfway around the globe by the people of Peru and Mexico.

A cotton fabric found in Peru dating from around 2200 B.C.

Woven cotton skirt from Peru, tenth to thirteenth centuries A.D.

In these two widely separated parts of the world, cotton must have grown wild. Then people learned to cultivate cotton plants in their fields.

American Indians were using cotton in the southwestern part of the United States about thirteen hundred years ago.

Page from a book showing ancient Mexican cotton textile designs, from fifteenth to sixteenth centuries A.D.

Part of an Arabic cotton garment, twelfth century A.D.

But this plant was not known in Europe until the time of Alexander the Great, who led large armies to the Far East in 327 B.C. He saw cotton being grown in India and came back with robes made of it. He also spread word of its use to the countries around the shores of the Mediterranean Sea.

In Europe, wool was the only fiber used to make clothing. Then from the Far East came tales of plants that grew "wool." Traders claimed that cotton was the wool of tiny animals, named Scythian lambs, that grew on the stalks of a plant. The stalks, each with a lamb as its flower, were said to bend over so the small sheep could graze on the grass around the plant. These fantastic stories were shown to be untrue when the Arabs brought the cotton plant to Spain in the Middle Ages.

Fanciful drawing of Scythian lambs by a German artist, fifteenth century A.D.

In the fourteenth century, cotton was shipped from the Mediterranean countries to mills in the Netherlands in northern Europe for spinning and weaving. Cotton could only grow where there were at least 180 days of warm weather and plenty of rain and sunlight.

From ancient times, cotton fibers were spun, that is, drawn out and twisted into a thread or strand of yarn, by hand. But, in 1765, the spinning jenny was invented by an Englishman named James Hargreaves. This machine was able to spin eight to eleven threads at the same time.

In 1769, Richard Arkwright, also English, introduced a roller spinning method, which pulled and twisted the yarn and wound it on large spools in one operation.

Until the mid eighteenth century, cotton was not manufactured in England, because the wool manufacturers there did not want it to compete with their own product. They had managed to pass a law in 1720 making the manufacture or sale of cotton cloth illegal. When the law was finally repealed in 1736, cotton mills grew in number.

spinning jenny

Cotton mills could not be established in the United States as the English would not allow any of the machinery to leave the country because they feared the colonies would compete with them. But a man named Samuel Slater, who had worked in a mill in England, was able to build an American cotton mill from memory in 1790.

13

Before cotton fibers could be spun into thread or yarn for making cloth, the seeds had to be separated from them. This work was very time-consuming. In 1793, an American inventor named Eli Whitney

cotton gin

changed the way cotton was produced when he invented a machine known as the cotton gin. It separated the fiber from the seeds mechanically and saved many long hours of handwork. Separating one pound of lint from the seeds by hand was considered a good day's work. Whitney's gin was able to separate fifty pounds per day.

Since then, many improvements have been made in the processing of cotton, one of the most valued fibers in the world.

THE PLANT

Cotton is part of your daily life from the time you use a soft cotton towel in the morning until you go to bed on cotton sheets at night. In spite of synthetic fibers such as dacron, orlon, and nylon, half of the world's textiles are still made of cotton. It is the most important fiber plant in the world. The property that sets cotton apart from synthetics is the power to absorb moisture. It is also easily spun into cloth.

Here is a cotton plant. But where is the cotton? To find out, you must watch the development of the plant.

After a cotton seed is planted, the first two leaves appear. They are called "seed leaves," because they come from inside the seed. They provide food for the growing plant until it produces additional leaves.

The leaves that come later are the true leaves.

New leaves keep appearing until the plant looks like the one in the picture.

If you look at the leaves close up, you can see that they resemble maple leaves. On one branch, there is a flower bud forming.

The bud is covered by fringed leaflike parts called "bracts."

In this picture, the bud is pushing its way out.

Now it is opening.

Here the flower is wide open. What a beautiful
flower on such a useful plant!
But there is no cotton yet.

The cotton flower looks very much like the pink mallow flowers that grow in swampy areas. They are relatives and belong in the same plant family.

When the petals are pulled off, you can see
the sexual parts of the flower—the stamens and
the pistil.

The stamens, the male parts of the flower, are
joined together into a column.

When the sacs on the top of the stamens open,
you can see the pollen grains.

POLLEN GRAIN

If you remove all the stamens and the petals, you can see the pistil, the female part of the flower. The pistil has three parts—the stigma at the top, the ovary at the bottom, and a connecting style in between.

STIGMA

STYLE

OVARY

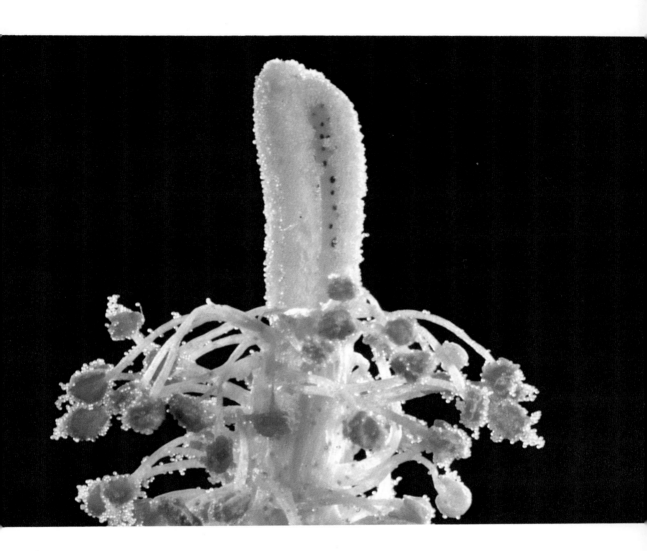

While the column of stamens is still in place in the
flower, the stigma grows through the center of it.

Pollen from the stamens must be transferred to the stigma of the flower in order for the ovary to develop into a cotton boll. Insects may transfer the pollen, but cotton flowers also can pollinate themselves.

Each pollen grain sends a tube down through the style to the ovary where there are ovules, or "seeds-to-be." The ovules become seeds if they are fertilized, or joined by the contents of a pollen grain.

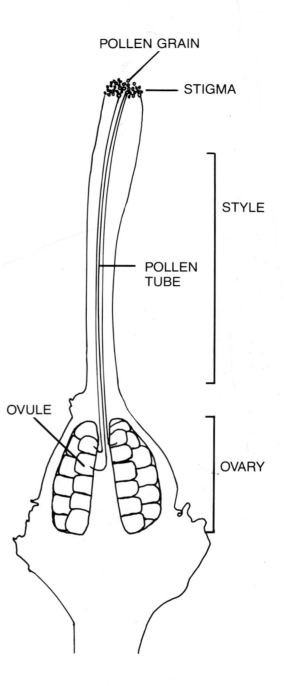

POLLEN GRAIN

STIGMA

STYLE

POLLEN TUBE

OVULE

OVARY

Around the seeds, the ovary will then swell into a boll. The boll is classified as a fruit because it contains seeds.

The flowers remain open for only a short time. Usually they bloom in the morning. They must be pollinated the same day, because in the afternoon they begin to wither and turn pink. The next morning they are rose-colored and withered. Then they quickly fall from the plant.

Children in cotton-growing areas in the South sometimes sing this song about the flowers:

First day white,
next day red,
third day from my birth
  —I'm dead.

As the petals dry and fall off, the ovary begins to change into a boll.

Meanwhile, the leaves turn red.

The boll gets bigger and bigger.

Finally, in about four months, the boll begins to split open.

At last you can see cotton. It is inside the boll.

In the pictures on the opposite page, the cotton is pulled out of the boll to show the seeds.

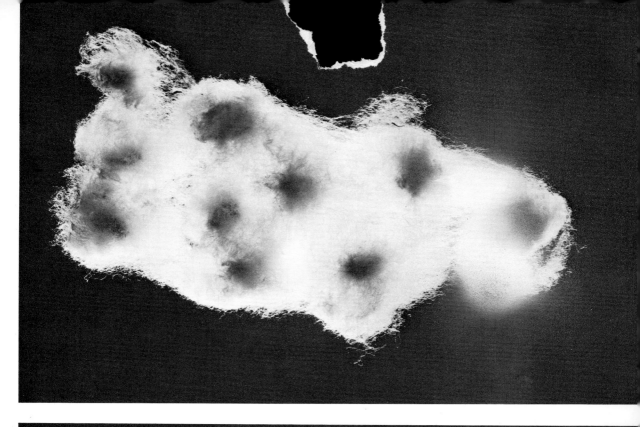

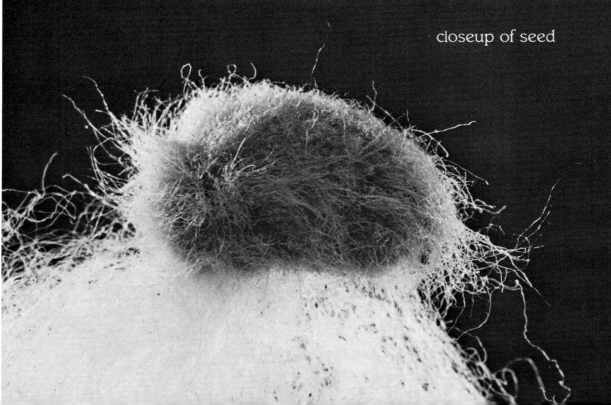

closeup of seed

The cotton fibers are actually hairs that grow out of the seed coats. Each seed has about 10,000 to 20,000 fibers.

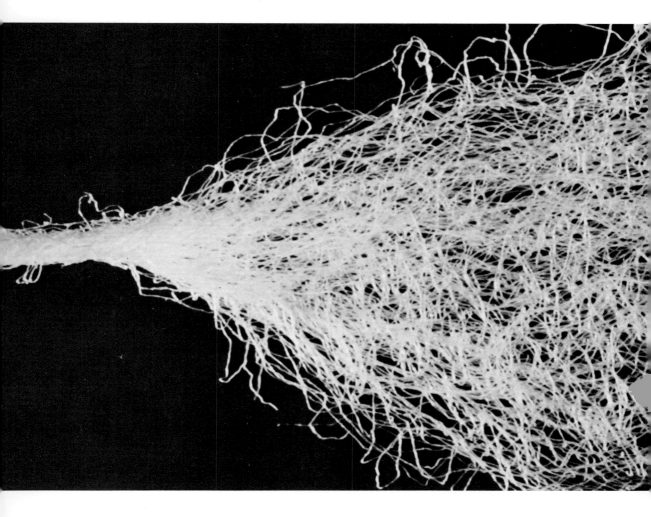

After the boll matures, the fibers die and lose water. Each fiber collapses into what looks like a twisted ribbon. Now the cotton fiber can easily be spun or twisted into thread.

enlarged over 2,000 times

The cotton bolls are ready for harvesting.

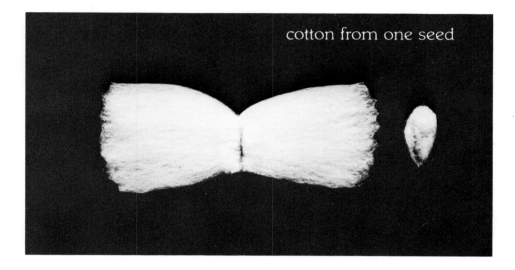

cotton from one seed

PROCESSING

Here is a field of cotton ready to be picked. Before machinery was invented to do the job, this work was done by hand. Now giant mechanical cotton pickers harvest the fields. They remove the cotton and seeds from the bolls.

The cotton is taken to the cotton gin. Inside the gin, the fiber and seeds are separated. The seeds come out in one place and the cotton in another.

Cotton seeds are rich in oil. The oil is pressed out of them and is used for salad oil, margarine, and in the manufacture of soaps and cosmetics. What is left of the seeds is rich in protein and makes good cattle food.

A certain amount of seed, however, is always kept for planting a new crop.

The cotton fiber is packed in bales and taken to the textile mill. The long hairs called "lint" can be spun into thread for making cloth. There are short hairs too. They are called "fuzz" and are used to make cotton batting, rayon, various types of plastics, and other products.

At the textile mill, a machine opens the bales and sends the cotton through a system of chutes and pipes to the carding machine. Inside the carding machine, big rollers with wire teeth comb the fibers so that they all lie more or less in the same direction. Then the fibers are pulled through a narrow opening like a funnel. The cotton fibers now look like long ropes. These ropes are called "slivers." In this picture, the rope is being wound into a large can at the left.

This photograph shows several strands of sliver in the process of being combined and drawn out to form a single strand.

Then the cotton goes to a roving machine, which twists the ropelike slivers, draws them out into thinner strands, and winds them on bobbins. They are now called "roving."

The roving is further drawn and lightly twisted into yarn. This process is called "ring spinning."

Another, more recent process called "open-end spinning" sends the sliver into a machine that twists it directly into yarn.

The yarn is then wound onto large spools that are placed on the looms for weaving.

The yarn on the loom that runs lengthwise is called the "warp yarn." The yarn that runs crosswise is called the "filling yarn."

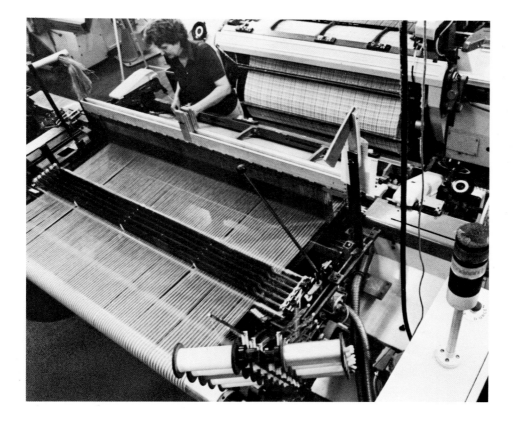

In this weaving room, you can see the end product—cotton cloth.

The fact that cotton absorbs moisture and allows it to evaporate easily makes it a perfect fiber for sport clothes and jeans, as well as astronauts' in-flight space suits. This property also makes it ideal for underwear, bed linen, and towels. Cotton is durable too. Cotton clothing is easy to wash and can be laundered over and over again without damage to the fibers.

While many synthetics have been developed, none yet has all the good qualities found in cotton. This natural fiber is still unequaled.

INDEX

indicates illustration

Alexander the Great, 10
Arkwright, Richard, 12
bales, 41*
boll, 28, 29*, 30*, 32*, 33*, 34*, 37, 38
bracts, 20*
carding machine, 41
cloth, cotton, 46*; properties of, 47; uses of, 47. *See also* fabric, textiles
cotton: development of plant, 16*-37*; discovery of, 7-11; flower, 19*-23*; importance of, 15, 47; leaves, 17*-19*; processing, 38-47; products, 41; properties of, 15, 47; sexual parts, 24*-28*
cotton gin, 14*, 15, 40*
cultivation, 12
fabric, 7*, 8*, 10*. *See also* cotton cloth
fertilization, 28
fibers, 12, 36*, 37*, 41-42
flowers, 19*, 20*, 21*, 22*, 23*, 24-30
fuzz, 41
Hargreaves, James, 12
harvesting, 38, 39*
leaves: seed, 17*; true, 17*, 18*
lint, 41
looms, 45*

mills, 12, 13
ovary, 26*, 29*, 30*
ovules, 28*
petal, 26
pistil, 24, 26*
pollen grains, 25*, 28*
pollination, 28, 29; with insects, 28
processing, 38-47; by hand, 12-15; mechanical, 38, 39*, 40*, 42*, 43*, 44*, 45*, 46*
roving machine, 43*, 44*
sacs, 25*
Scythian lambs, 11*
seed coats, 36*
seed oil, 40
seeds, 14, 34, 35*, 38*
Slater, Samuel, 13
slivers, 24*, 43*, 44
spinning, 12; open-end, 44*; ring, 44*; roller, 12
spinning jenny, 12, 13*
stamen, 24*, 25*, 26, 27*, 28*
stigma, 26*, 27*, 28*
style, 26*, 28*
textiles, 9*, 15, 41
weaving, 12, 45*, 46*
Whitney, Eli, 14
wool, 11, 12
yarn, 12, 44, 45; warp, 45; filling, 45

48